What was it like in the past?

People at work

Louise and Richard Spilsbury

www.heinemann.co.uk/library
Visit our website to find out more information about Heinemann Library books.

To order:
☎ Phone 44 (0) 1865 888066
 Send a fax to 44 (0) 1865 314091
 Visit the Heinemann Bookshop at www.heinemann.co.uk/library to browse our catalogue and order online.

First published in Great Britain by Heinemann Library, Halley Court, Jordan Hill, Oxford OX2 8EJ, a division of Reed Educational and Professional Publishing Ltd. Heinemann is a registered trademark of Reed Educational & Professional Publishing Ltd.

OXFORD MELBOURNE AUCKLAND JOHANNESBURG BLANTYRE
GABORONE IBADAN PORTSMOUTH (NH) USA CHICAGO

© Reed Educational and Professional Publishing Ltd 2003
The moral right of the proprietor has been asserted.

All rights reserved. No part of this publication may be reproduced, stored in a retrieval system, or transmitted in any form or by any means, electronic, mechanical, photocopying, recording, or otherwise without either the prior written permission of the Publishers or a licence permitting restricted copying in the United Kingdom issued by the Copyright Licensing Agency Ltd, 90 Tottenham Court Road, London W1P 0LP.

Designed by Celia Floyd
Originated by Ambassador Litho Ltd
Printed in Hong Kong/China

ISBN 0 431 14822 8   (hardback)   ISBN 0 431 14832 5   (paperback)
07 06 05 04 03   07 06 05 04 03
10 9 8 7 6 5 4 3 2 1   10 9 8 7 6 5 4 3 2 1

British Library Cataloguing in Publication Data
Spilsbury, Louise
    People at work. – (What was it like in the past?)
    1. Occupations – History – Juvenile literature 2. Work
    I. Title II.Spilsbury, Richard
    331.1'25'09

Acknowledgements
The Publishers would like to thank the following for permission to reproduce photographs:
Beamish Museum Archive: 11; Hulton Archive: 4, 6, 8, 12, 15, 16, 17, 20; Impact: Francesca Yorke: 26, Piers Cavendish 27, Simon Shepheard 24, 25; John Walmsley: 29; Mary Evans: 9, 10; Popperfoto: 14, 18, 19; Powerstock Zefa: 28; Topham: 5, 7, 13, 21, 22, 23.

Our thanks to Stuart Copeman for his help in the preparation of this book.

Cover photograph reproduced with permission of Hulton.

Every effort has been made to contact copyright holders of any material reproduced in this book. Any omissions will be rectified in subsequent printings if notice is given to the Publisher.

Contents

Then and now	4
1900s: Farming and fishing	6
1900s: Factory work	8
1910s: Work in service	10
1910s: Women at work	12
1920s: Coal and electricity	14
1930s: Out of work	16
1940s: War work	18
1950s: Doctors and teachers	20
1960s and 1970s: Fashion and fun	22
1980s: Buying and selling	24
1990s: Working with computers	26
2000s: Work today	28
Find out for yourself	30
Glossary	31
Index	32

Words printed in **bold letters like these** are explained in the Glossary.

Each **decade** is highlighted on a timeline at the bottom of the page.

Then and now

What do you think of when you see or hear the word 'work'? Perhaps you think of what you do at school, or what grown-ups do when you are there. In this book, work means the jobs people do to earn money.

Look at the food shops on these two pages. What differences can you see?

In 1907, this man was selling fruit and vegetables from nearby farms.

This modern supermarket sells all kinds of food from all over the world.

In 1900, a shopkeeper served the customers and added up the prices of the things they bought on a piece of paper. Today, people pick things off the shelves themselves and computers do all the adding up.

This book looks at some of the other ways work has changed over the last 100 years.

1900s: Farming and fishing

In the countryside in the 1900s, most people worked on farms. They grew food to eat and to sell. Very few farmers had machines like tractors. They used oxen or horses to pull the ploughs (tools which dug the soil). Farmers did many jobs by hand, such as cutting **crops** or loading them onto carts.

In the 1900s many farmers used horses to pull their ploughs.

1900   1910   1920   1930   1940

Fishermen set out on boats every morning and evening to catch fish.

Many people worked in fishing around the coast of Britain. Today, fishing boats can go far out to sea because they have big refrigerators on board to keep the fish fresh. In the 1900s, fishing boats did not go out so far because they had to bring the fish back sooner.

1900s: Factory work

In the 1900s, many people who lived in towns and cities worked in **factories**. Lots of people worked long hours and the **wages** were low.

> Many people did not earn enough money to buy much food for their families. One woman remembered:
>
> 'My mother went without herself for us, yes. I've known her wipe the plate round with a drop of gravy, and tell my father she'd had her dinner, she'd never had any.'

Women in this hat factory worked six days a week and until 10 o'clock at night.

In some places nearly all people worked in one **industry**. For example, in Sheffield most men worked in factories making **steel**. Some men shovelled coal into hot ovens, which were used to melt the steel. Others used machines to beat the steel into shape.

In this steel factory in Sheffield, hot metal was shaped into new objects.

1910s: Work in service

In the 1910s, many people worked **in service**. This meant that they worked as **servants** for rich people. Servants did all the work around a house.

At this time most girls and boys finished school when they were 12 or 14 years old. Many of them left their families and went to live in a big house to work as a servant.

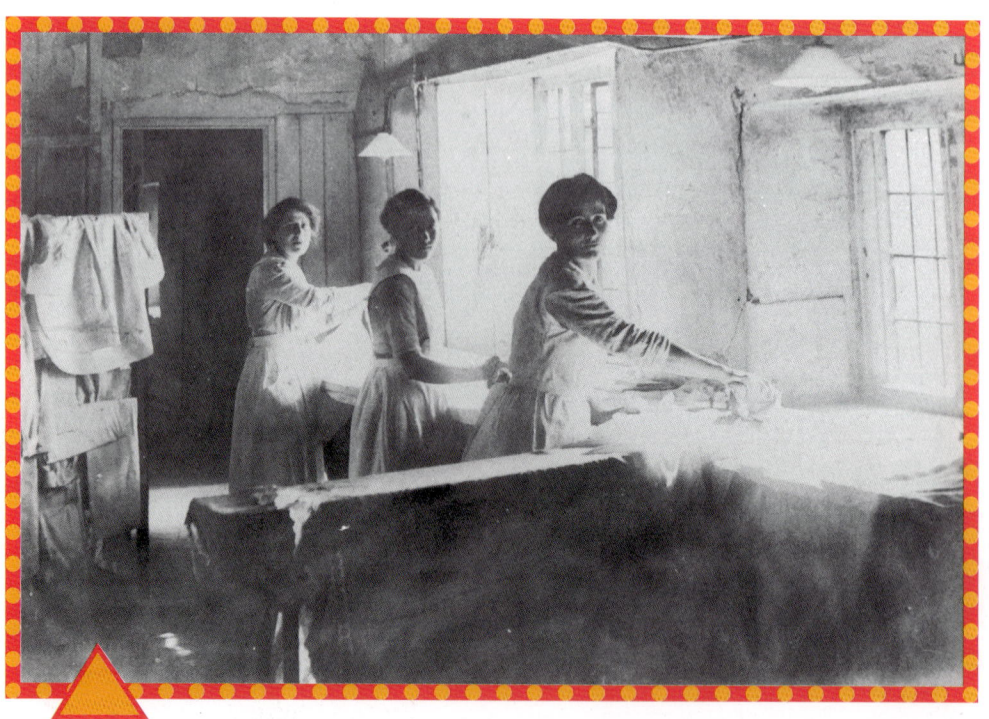

Doing the laundry was one of the many tasks young servants had to carry out.

Men usually had different jobs to women. In big houses, some men were butlers. They told the other servants what to do. Some men looked after the gardens.

Women mostly did the housework and cooking. Some looked after the rich family's children. Some were maids who helped rich people get dressed.

Servants who worked in a big house in 1910.

1910s: Women at work

In the 1910s, not many women went out to work. Some worked **in service** or in **factories**, and a few were schoolteachers. Most married women were not supposed to work at all. They were expected to stay at home and look after their house and children.

In the 1910s some women were school teachers.

During the war women tried lots of jobs they had not done before, like road building.

From 1914 until 1918 Britain was at war with Germany. This was called the First World War. Many men left their jobs to fight as soldiers in Europe. Women had to take over some of their jobs. Women delivered post and drove ambulances. Some worked in factories making guns and **bombs** for the war.

1920s: Coal and electricity

In the 1920s, most people burned coal to heat their homes and stoves. Coal comes from underground **mines**. Coal miners had the job of digging out the coal. Others then sorted it and loaded it onto trucks. When it reached the surface other people took it away on trains or boats to sell.

Coal miners worked in cramped, dark tunnels. They got bad coughs from breathing in the dust from the coal.

In the 1920s electricity was used in some **factories** and homes for the first time. Lots of people found work in the special factories that made electricity. Other people found work making, selling or mending the new electric gadgets that were invented, such as electric irons and typewriters.

In the 1920s only richer people could afford electric machines, like this typewriter.

1930s: Out of work

In the 1930s, nearly a quarter of all people who could work had no jobs. People without work are said to be **unemployed**. At this time there were fewer jobs in **industries** like farming and coalmining. The **government** paid unemployed people some money to help them but they were still very poor.

These people do not have jobs. They are waiting in line to be given a small amount of money to help them buy food.

*In the 1930s men began to use machines to help them build cars in a **factory**.*

Before the 1930s, most cars were made by hand and were too expensive for most people to buy. Now lots were being made at one time with the help of machines. This made the cars cheaper so more people could now afford to buy them. Some people also found work in new garages.

1940s: War work

Between 1939 and 1945, Britain was at war with Germany. This war was called the Second World War. Many women did 'war work', such as making **bombs**.

An 18-year-old girl who worked in a bomb factory said: 'Working in a **factory** was not fun. To be shut in for hours on end, with not even a window to see daylight, was grim... I think boredom was our worst enemy.'

During the war, women took over many of the jobs usually done by men.

Can you imagine what it must have been like when a street was bombed?

Many men went to fight in the war. Some were too old and others were not fit enough. Some of these men worked as **air raid** wardens. Their job was to call fire engines to put out fires caused by the bombs. The warden also checked if anyone was injured and called an ambulance to help them.

1950s: Doctors and teachers

Before the 1950s, most people had to pay to see a doctor. Many could not afford it so did not go. By the 1950s everyone could visit a doctor for free. More people **trained** to be doctors than ever before.

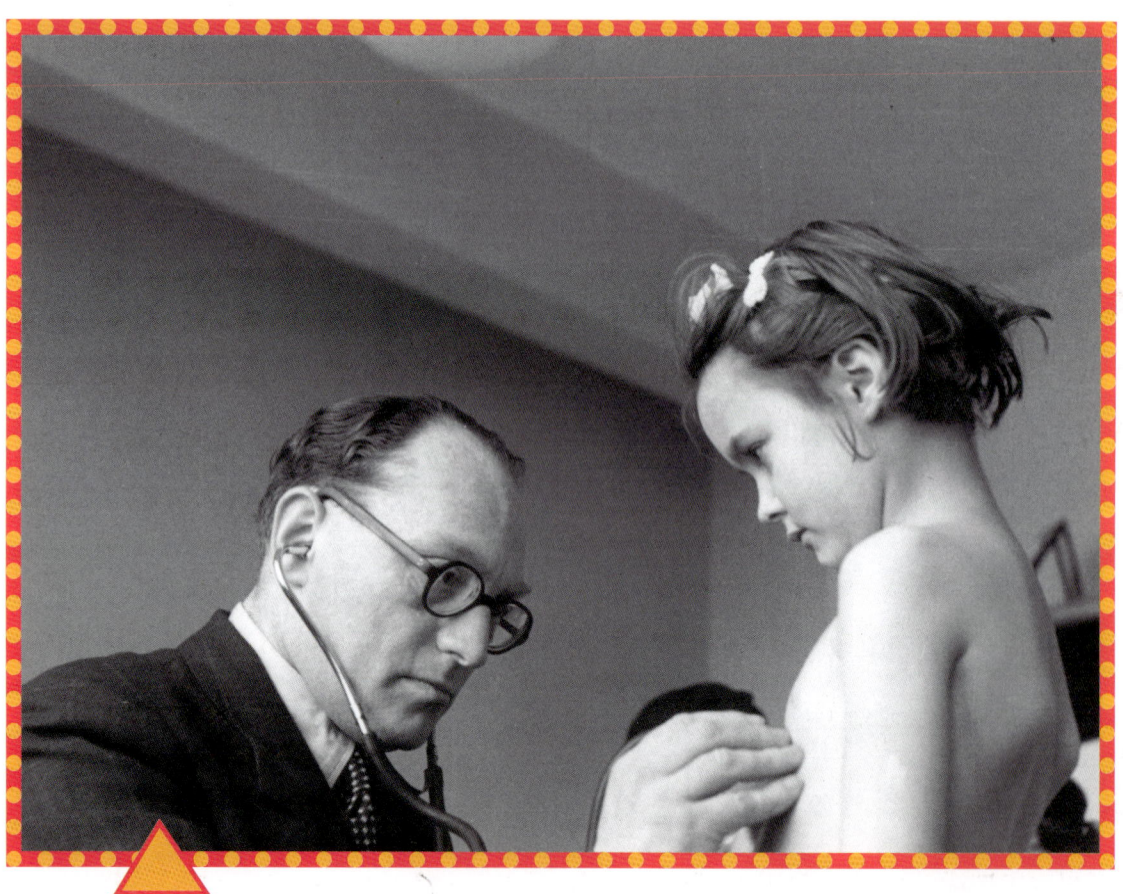

This doctor is trying to find out why the little girl feels ill.

How are these school uniforms different to those people wear today?

After the Second World War, lots more schools were built in Britain. This was partly because there were more children than ever before. Also, by the 1950s all children had to go to school until they were 15. More people were trained as teachers for the new schools.

1960s and 1970s: Fashion and fun

In the 1960s people had more free time and more money to spend than before. Fashion became a big business. Fashion is the way people dress.

Lots of people worked in the fashion **industry**. Many made clothes in **factories**. Some worked in shops selling the clothes. Others wrote about fashion in magazines and newspapers.

This street is full of shops selling fashionable clothes in the 1960s.

In the 1970s, people had more time and money to spend on holidays too. Lots of people work in the holiday **industry**. Think about a holiday by the sea. Plane, train or coach drivers take you there. At a hotel, someone cleans your room and makes your food. When you go out, there are other people working in cafés and shops.

How many different jobs can you think of at a holiday spot like this?

1980s: Buying and selling

How do you choose what to buy with your pocket money? Perhaps you see things you like in adverts on television. In the 1980s lots of people worked in **advertising**. Advertisers think up ideas for adverts, film the adverts or write the music to go with them.

This worker is sticking up a giant advertising poster.

Lots of people work for shops all over the country.

What about the people who sell things? By the 1980s, many people worked in chainstores. Chainstores are shops with the same name in towns all over the country. Some shop workers sell to customers. Others deliver the things to sell and put them on the shelves.

1990s: Working with computers

By the 1990s computers were making a huge difference to people's jobs. For example, computers made it possible for more people to work from home. People can do their work on their computers at home and send it to another computer in an office.

If you have an office at home, you save a lot of time because you do not have to travel to work.

What differences can you see between this factory and the factories on page 8 and 17?

In the 1990s more **factories** used computers and robots to make things. Robots are machines that do some of the jobs people can do. People use computers to tell robots what to do. They write special instructions that tell the robots how to move.

2000s: Work today

In 1900 most people worked using their hands to make or do things. Today machines do a lot of the work. In the past there were a lot of jobs women were not supposed to do. Now they can do almost any job they want to. At one time, most people worked near where they lived. Now people travel all over the world to work.

Some computers are so small you can sit them on your lap and do your work while you are on a plane!

Some jobs are much the same today as they were in the past. Many postmen and women still ride bicycles to deliver post, just as they did long ago.

What jobs can you think of that people do today that they also did in the past?

Teachers still sit or stand at the front of a class and explain new ideas to children.

Find out for yourself

There are lots of ways you can find out about the past. You could start by asking your parents, grandparents or even your great-grandparents what jobs they have had and what they remember about them.

Ask people you know if they have any photographs of themselves at work in the past. Older photographs will be in black and white, but they can tell you a lot about what jobs people did in the past and what tools or machines people used.

Books

History from Photographs: People Who Help Us, Hodder Wayland, 1999
History Mysteries: Farming, A & C Black, 1992

Glossary

advertising when people make adverts to try to persuade other people to buy things

air raid when enemy planes dropped bombs on towns and cities

bombs when bombs hit the ground they explode and destroy everything nearby

crops plants that are grown for food, such as potatoes

decade ten years. The decade of the 1910s means the ten years between 1910 and 1920

factories big buildings where lots of people work together using machines to make things

government group of people who make important decisions about how the country is run

industry kind of work. The car industry means all the people who make and sell cars.

in service when people worked as servants in other people's homes

mines deep holes made by people so they can go underground to dig and collect coal

servants people who work for (serve) others in their homes doing jobs like cooking and cleaning

steel a kind of metal that was used to make things, such as knives and forks

trained taught to do something

unemployed when a person does not have a job

wages money paid for doing a job

Index

advertising 24
air raid wardens 19
bombs 13, 18, 19
cars 17
coalmining 14, 16
computers 5, 26, 27
crops 6
doctor 20
electricity 15
factories 8, 9, 12, 15, 18, 22, 27
farming 4, 6, 16
fashion 22
First World War 13
fishing 7
industry 9, 16, 17, 22
schoolteachers 12, 21, 29
Second World War 18, 21
servants 10, 11
shopworkers 4, 5, 22, 25
soldiers 13
steel 9
women 12, 13, 18, 28